SHAPED BY SCRIPTURE

Who Do You Say I Am?

LUKE

DAN BOONE AND AMY BOONE

2

Copyright © 2022 by The Foundry Publishing®
The Foundry Publishing®
PO Box 419527
Kansas City, MO 64141
thefoundrypublishing.com

978-0-8341-4105-6

Printed in the
United States of America

Cover and Interior Design: J. R. Caines
Layout: Jeff Gifford

All Scripture quotations, unless indicated, are taken from THE HOLY BIBLE, NEW
INTERNATIONAL VERSION®, NIV® Copyright © 1973, 1978, 1984, 2011 by Biblica,
Inc.® Used by permission. All rights reserved worldwide.

The internet addresses, email addresses, and phone numbers in this book are
accurate at the time of publication. They are provided as a resource. The Foundry
Publishing does not endorse them or vouch for their content or permanence.

10 9 8 7 6 5 4 3 2 1

Contents

3

THE *SHAPED BY SCRIPTURE* SERIES

The first step of an organized study of the Bible is the selection of a biblical book, which is not always an easy task. Often people pick a book they are already familiar with, books they think will be easy to understand, or books that, according to popular opinion, seem to have more relevance to Christians today than other books of the Bible. However, it is important to recognize the truth that God's Word is not limited to just a few books. All the biblical books, both individually and collectively, communicate God's Word to us. As Paul affirms in 2 Timothy 3:16, "All Scripture is God-breathed and is useful for teaching, rebuking, correcting and training in righteousness." We interpret the term "God-breathed" to mean inspired by God. If Christians are going to take 2 Timothy 3:16 seriously, then we should all set the goal of encountering God's Word as communicated through all sixty-six books of the Bible.

By purchasing this volume, you have chosen to study the Gospel of Luke, which is one of four Gospels in the New Testament. The Gospels portray the life of Jesus in unique ways depending on their authors. The author of Matthew's Gospel is concerned with encouraging and instructing Jewish Christians in their adjusted religious lives. Mark's goal is to present Jesus as heroic and action-oriented, and to remind his readers that the powerful Son of God was also crucified. The author of John's Gospel is primarily concerned with presenting an enhanced vision of the salvation that is available to all through Jesus the Messiah, who was the true, incarnate Son of God. Luke's particular emphasis is on Jesus's interest in the socially marginalized, and on calling sinners and religious insiders to repentance. The goal of this series is to illustrate an appropriate method of studying the Bible, so this volume will focus on seven specific scenes and events from the life of Jesus as depicted by Luke, with the hope that the method modeled and practiced here will give you a useful way to engage further study.

How This Study Works

This Bible study is intended for a period of seven weeks. We have chosen a specific passage for each week's study. This study can be done individually or with a small group.

For individual study, we recommend a five-day study each week, following the guidelines given below:

1 On the first day of the study, read the relevant passage several times until you become fully familiar with the verses, words, and phrases.

2 On the second day, we will review the setting and organization of the passage.

3 On the third day, we will observe some of the realities portrayed in the passage.

4 On the fourth day, we will investigate the relationship of the individual passage to the larger story of God in the Bible.

5 On the fifth day, we will reflect on the function of the story as we hear it today, the invitation it extends to us, and our response to God, who speaks through God's Word.

If this Bible study is done as a group activity, we recommend that members of the group meet together on the sixth day to share and discuss what they have learned from God's Word and how it has transformed their lives.

You may want to
have a study Bible to
give you additional
insights as we work
through the Gospel
of Luke. Other
helpful resources are
*Discovering the New
Testament* and two
volumes of *Luke: A
Commentary in the
Wesleyan Tradition*,
available from The
Foundry Publishing.

6

Literary Forms in the Bible

There are several literary forms represented throughout the Bible. The divinely inspired writers used various techniques to communicate God's Word to their ancient audiences. The major literary forms (also known as genres) of the Bible are:

- narratives

- laws

- history

- Wisdom literature (in the form of dialogues and proverbial statements)

- poetry (consisting of poems of praise, lament, trust in God, and more)

- prophecy

- discourses

- parables

- miracle stories

- letters (also known as epistles)

- exhortations

- apocalyptic writings

Within each of these forms, one may find subgenres. Each volume in the *Shaped by Scripture* series will briefly overview the genres found in the book of the Bible that is the subject of that study.

When biblical writers utilized a particular literary form, they intended for it to have a specific effect on their audience. This concept can be understood by examining genres that are familiar to us in our contemporary setting. For example, novels that are comedies inspire good and happy feelings in their readers; tragedies, on the other hand, are meant to induce sorrow. What is true of the intended effect of literary forms in contemporary literature is also true of literary forms found in the Bible.

THE GOSPEL OF LUKE

Luke is the street-corner newsboy of the New Testament. And his Gospel is the news—the good news about Jesus. It's an out-in-the-open, meant-for-everyone, come-and-get-it, read-all-about-it kind of news. It's an expanded invitation. Luke's Gospel takes stories and traditions and good news and puts them all where God has always intended—in the hands of *everyone*.

Who Wrote Luke?

Both external (outside the Bible) and internal (inside the Bible) evidence exists that allows us to name the author of the third Gospel in the New Testament as Luke. Though the name Luke does not appear in the Gospel, multiple early references outside the Bible directly or indirectly attribute the work to a physician named Luke. Additionally, references found elsewhere in the Bible point to Luke as a close companion of Paul. See, for example, Colossians 4:14, 2 Timothy 4:11, and Philemon 1:24, which all reference Luke.

While much of the content of Mark, Matthew, and Luke is similar, Luke's perspective is unique as a physician and well-educated gentile. His profession leads us naturally to assume that he would hold himself to high standards with regard to research and writing. We expect Luke to uncover and record the stories of Christ with the thoroughness and attention of a doctor—someone who is interested in accuracy, care, and healing. Luke is a problem-solution writer. He sees the sin and brokenness of all of humanity, and he offers his stories as proof that Jesus is the solution.

Audience

Part of what makes Luke's Gospel so beautiful, and part of why it resonates so strongly with us today, is that it carries the good news to a new audience—the non-Jewish people referred to as the gentiles. Luke says the message he is relaying is for everyone. The Jews no longer hold a monopoly on the good news; it is now available to all, in the form of the accessible letters and stories written by Luke and passed from hand to hand, circulating, spreading, reaching ever farther.

Literary Form

Luke's Gospel doesn't begin with the stories he has collected of Jesus. It begins by placing Jesus in the historic lineage of the Old Testament. The Jewish story starts with the Jews, but in the promise of Abraham, it extends to every tribe and nation. Luke will tell more of this story in his sequel to the Gospel, the Acts of the Apostles. We have hints of where this story is headed in the Gospel. His writing doesn't just nod to the Old Testament—it begins with it, rests on it, and now interprets it through the lens of Jesus Christ. This New Testament Gospel is not the beginning of a new story; it's the continuation of an old one: the great love story between Creator God and all of his creation.

Written late in the first century, probably around the year 80, Luke is one of three synoptic Gospels (Matthew and Mark being the other two). These three Gospels, particularly Luke and Matthew, have large chunks of material that are similar or even identical in wording, leading some to believe that a single source (possibly Mark) was used or referenced, and then expounded upon, in the writing of each Gospel. However, some of the more popular stories we know are found only in Luke: Gabriel's visit to Mary, the good Samaritan, the prodigal son, and Zacchaeus, among others. In all, there are fourteen parables that are unique to Luke's Gospel.

But how should we read Luke's Gospel? In any written work, it's important to consider the rhetorical methods of the writer. For Luke, the term "salvation" means more than being saved from sin. It is the liberation of people from disease, prejudice, poverty, sexism, religious judgment, and societal shame. With that in mind, we read his stories with the understanding that they were written to persuade readers to repent and turn to Christ. While it is a quasi-historical account addressed to Theophilus, it is more than an accurate reporting of the facts. It is good news that saves. Rhetorically, this Gospel is more like an infomercial than an encyclopedia. This understanding allows us to read Luke through a literary lens in which stories are shared specifically to affect and move readers, rather than a purely historical lens in which the sole purpose is factually accurate documentation.

A brief word should also be said about the companion volume to Luke, the Acts of the Apostles. Acts stands alone in the New Testament in a special way. It is like the four Gospels in telling stories of healings, teachings, demonic confrontations, opposition from enemies, imprisonments, and death. And it is like the epistles in visiting and addressing different cities with their named leaders, their local cultures, and their theological problems. Yet Acts is neither Gospel nor epistle. Similar to Luke, it is a theological narrative.

A narrative is a story. Stories cohere around characters who have experiences. Stories require a scaffolding of meaning. Stories need a setting with culture, language, and history. The more we understand the scaffolding around the story, the more we understand the story. We become insiders who share things in common with the characters in the story. The pure historian seeks to help people know what happened at a specific time and place. A historian's objectivity is important. They should seek to write without prejudice or opinion. They interview eyewitnesses, search documents, and look for evidence that fills in chronological blanks.

Luke is doing something different. He begins with the end in mind. He intends to influence his readers. In a sense, his work is more akin to a historical novel—a story that uses the historical setting and the facts but reorganizes them to serve the purpose of the narrative. He selects and arranges the events and tells them from his perspective. Luke becomes the omniscient narrator who is able to tell us the thoughts of the characters, put words into their mouths, and fill in the colors of their personalities. Even more important, Luke owns a theology, and he wants to persuade his readers to believe what he believes. His story is a theological narrative.

A good storyteller uses several devices. Repetition is one of them. There are connections between the stories of Luke and the stories of Acts. What we see Jesus do in Luke, we see the disciples repeat in Acts, from healings to casting out demons to confronting authorities to dying. Luke also repeats key words and phrases: boldness, signs and wonders, end of the earth, kingdom of God.

Another rhetorical device is the use of speeches made by the key characters. Jesus makes several speeches in Luke's Gospel in the form of parables, sermons, and responses to questions. Almost a third of Acts is speeches. The simple realities of papyrus, ink, and quill cause us to assume that no one was taking dictation when key speeches were made. But, similar to the Old Testament oral tradition, the early church recalled the sermons, sayings, and stories of Jesus until there was a fluid consensus about what he said.

Major Theological Themes

Woven into the twenty-four chapters of Luke's Gospel are several theological themes, including:

 God is on a mission. Luke's Gospel is a prelude to Acts, a theological narrative that recounts the spread of the gospel and the transition of the people of God from a dominantly Jewish community to a mission that extends to the ends of the earth. We cannot achieve a multinational, multiethnic people of God without meeting the Jesus of Luke's Gospel. Luke wants us to know that God has always been going to the whole world, to all people, to the ends of the earth—and now God has become flesh through Jesus of Nazareth.

 The kingdom of God is real and present on earth. The kingdom of God is a realm, a reality, a sphere, an environment that is filled with the uncontested presence of God. Theological geography is important here. We are not *down here* and the kingdom of God *way off up there*. We are here, and the kingdom is also here. It is not always visible, but sometimes it does break into the visible realm to make a dramatic difference. The kingdom of God has come among us in the person of Jesus Christ. He is here, and the kingdom is here in him.

 The Holy Spirit is real and active. We find in Luke a robust theology of the work of the Holy Spirit. God is more than an ancient being who started things and then stepped back. The nature and intent of God are understood through the work of the Holy Spirit. The Spirit energizes Jesus in the Gospel of Luke. Divine power and presence are unleashed in him as a blessing to all people.

God has made an invitation, and the people are expected to respond. In Luke's Gospel, invitation comes in the form of God's redemption—that brokenness can be fixed. The diagnostic tone of Luke's theology should not surprise us. We should expect that a doctor would be concerned with healing. Luke has great hope that humans can be healed and redeemed. The call for repentance echoes throughout the Gospel, and we see the human response to that invitation: people repent and believe and follow.

Luke explores the relationship between vulnerability and hospitality. Many of the stories in Luke's Gospel portray people and situations of extreme vulnerability. Perhaps better than any of the other Gospel writers, Luke the physician understands human frailty. But Luke also demonstrates a keen ability to celebrate the hospitality of God through the welcome of Jesus. The excluded find a home in Luke's reversal-of-fortune stories. Luke invites us into his theological narrative just as we are and offers us the hospitality of God's kingdom.

LUKE 2:1–40

We are vulnerable, and we know it. We have seen high-tech space shuttles disintegrate, skyscrapers collapse, stock markets plummet, marriages crumble, diseases spread, and countries at war. Any serious person who thinks about the way the world is and where it seems to be headed has reason to feel vulnerable. And we do all kinds of things to cope with our vulnerability, including overindulging in mindless entertainment that can make us numb to reality, or overscheduling ourselves to avoid serious thought, or over-insulating ourselves against potential risks and dangers. Instead of ignoring or avoiding our vulnerability, we should confront it by reading the story of Jesus's birth, which is filled to the brim with God's own vulnerability.

Luke's Gospel begins with the incarnation—the moment when God enters fully into our humanity and suffers with, for, and in us. It's a story of vulnerability. It is a moment when God leaves heaven to enter Mary's womb. As Luke's Gospel narrative unfolds and follows the story of Christ, we will be shown the full extent of this vulnerability, and perhaps it will help us come to grips with our own vulnerable state.

WEEK 1, DAY 1

Listen to the story in Luke 2:1–40 by reading it aloud several times until you become familiar with its verses, words, and phrases. Enjoy the experience of imagining the story in your mind, picturing each event as it unfolds.

WEEK 1, DAY 2

LUKE 2:1-40

The Setting

In Luke 1, we have seen the birth of John the Baptist to a barren Elizabeth and mute Zechariah. Similar to the story of Abraham and Sarah, God brings life to a dead womb. This is in character with the God who brings life from death and creates a future where there was none. John becomes the bearer of the news of the kingdom of God. The tender text of the visit between older Elizabeth, the best of old Israel, and betrothed Mary, the mother of the coming Messiah, is filled with hope and promise. In Mary's song (vv. 46–55) and Zechariah's prophecy (vv. 68–79), we hear the ancient hopes of Israel poured out as a prelude to the most-read story of Christmas—the Lukan account of Jesus's birth. Everything in Luke 1 has readied us for the announcement of the new King.

The Plot

God leaves heaven to enter the human womb. Surely he will pick a woman of great standing and stature, one who is respected in society and from a prominent family—right? Nope. He chooses an ordinary young woman with no claim to fame. Okay, well at least he'll make sure to enter the world surrounded by people who will love him and bring acclaim to this momentous birth? Afraid not. Mary and Joseph and God-in-womb are at the mercy of strangers. They are completely reliant on others to provide the most basic of human needs. Surely at this point God will bring forth a rich citizen to set them up with the best birthing facility Bethlehem has to offer? Wrong again. The birth of Christ is stripped of all of the comforts and cares of home. God's first breath of human air likely contains scents of hay, animal poop, and damp earth.

The story of Jesus begins with a reliance on human hospitality. God has become us: Desperate. Needy. Flesh. Yet this vulnerable baby will grow up to meet the needs of all humanity. But there's something else we need to note here. In the story of the incarnation, the stars of the show are less than stellar: a woman who could be stoned for being pregnant by some means other than her husband, shepherds who are not trusted to bear public testimony, an aged widow who camps out in the temple like a beggar on a street holding up a "Jesus is coming soon" sign. The characters do not symbolize power and prestige. They reek of vulnerability. This is central to the Gospel of Luke. As he spreads the good news to those who have traditionally been outside of the promise, he reminds gentiles that Jesus knows what it's like to be an outsider, unwelcome, a misfit.

Summarize or paraphrase the general message or theme of each grouping of verses. Follow the pattern provided for Luke 2:1–3 and Luke 2:4–7.

1. Luke 2:1–3

A census is underway. Everyone is required to register for taxation in their ancestral home.

_____

2. Luke 2:4–7

The census means Joseph will need to travel to his hometown of Bethlehem. Mary, his

pregnant fiancée, travels with him. She goes into labor while they are in Bethlehem. But there

is no place for them to stay, so their baby boy is born in a place meant for animals.

_____

3. Luke 2:8–15

_____

_____

_____

_____

4. Luke 2:16–20

_____

_____

_____

_____

_____

5. Luke 2:21–24

_____

_____

_____

_____

_____

6. Luke 2:25–35

_____

_____

_____

_____

_____

_____

_____

_____

7. Luke 2:36–38

_____

_____

_____

_____

_____

_____

_____

_____

8. Luke 2:39–40

_____

_____

_____

_____

_____

_____

_____

_____

WEEK 1, DAY 3

What's Happening in the Story?

As we notice certain circumstances in the story, we will begin to see how they are similar to or different from the realities of our world. The story will become the lens through which we see the world in which we live today. In our study today, you may encounter words and/or phrases that are unfamiliar to you. Some of the particular words and translation choices for them have been explained in more detail in the **Word Study Notes**. If you are interested in even more help or detail, you can supplement this study with a Bible dictionary or other Bible study resource.

Luke 2:1–40 can be divided into three main sections: the account of Jesus's birth in verses 1-7, the response of shepherds and angels in verses 8–20, and Jesus's first trip to the temple in verses 21–40. **Jot down a summary description of the world and reality that is portrayed in the following verses. Follow the pattern provided for Luke 2:1–7 and Luke 2:21–40.**

1. Luke 2:1–7

Mary and Joseph travel from the town of Nazareth in Galilee, near the coast of the Mediterranean Sea, approximately eighty miles directly south to the town of Bethlehem in Judea. Mary and Joseph must make the trip as decreed by Emperor Caesar Augustus's Roman census to pay their taxes. Jesus is born in Bethlehem[1] and lies in a manger "because there is no room for them in the inn."[2]

17

WORD STUDY NOTES #1

[1] This inconvenient and seemingly ill-timed trip fulfills the prophesy of Micah 5:2, "But you, Bethlehem Ephrathah, though you are small among the clans of Judah, out of you will come for me one who will be ruler over Israel, whose origins are from of old, from ancient times."

[2] We've tended to Americanize the setting of the nativity. We picture a rustic barn with wind whistling through slatted boards. But this might not be accurate. The landscape of Bethlehem is peppered with many, many cave formations. In many instances, family animals were kept in a nearby cave, which would provide natural protection. It is likely that a family's animal cave was the setting for Christ's birth.

WORD STUDY NOTES #2

[1] While most of us might think of "glory" as synonymous with a blinding light, a better translation of the word might be the sense of being overwhelmed. The Hebrew root of "glory" is related more closely to our concept of heaviness, or weightiness. To be in awe of God's glory is to be overcome, weighed down, overwhelmed by his presence.

2. Luke 2:8–20[1]

_____

_____

_____

_____

_____

_____

_____

_____

WORD STUDY NOTES #3

[1] The naming of Jesus, as instructed by the angel, is the use of the ancient name Yeshua, or Joshua, which denotes the hope that "God saves." Jesus is named "the one who saves."

[2] The offering of a pair of turtledoves or two young pigeons is one of the hints we get about the economic status of the holy family. This is the sacrifice of a poor family.

[3] Do not miss the connection between the naming of Jesus and the testimony of Simeon. He holds in his arms the baby who has just been named "the one who saves," he recognizes the fulfillment of the Old Testament in the accompanying required sacrifice, and he responds by saying, "My eyes have seen God's salvation."

3. Luke 2:21–40

Mary and Joseph follow the customs of their day and faith, which include naming,[1] circumcision, dedication, and sacrifice.[2] These actions are expected of this young Jewish family. Then we meet Simeon, who has been waiting all his life to meet the promised Messiah. In fact, God has promised him that he won't die until he sees him. Luke doesn't give us many details about how the whole thing happens. We don't know how Simeon knows Jesus is the Messiah. We only know that he follows the guidance of the Holy Spirit to go to the temple and that he recognizes Jesus as soon as he sees him.[3] After Simeon, we meet Anna. Luke tells us four things about her: she is a prophet, she is old, she has been a widow for far longer than she was married, and she never leaves the temple. She sees the young family in the midst of their errand and, like Simeon, recognizes the Savior, preaching about him "to all who were looking forward to the redemption of Jerusalem."

Discoveries

Let's summarize our discoveries from Luke 2:1–40.

1. Our understanding of Jesus must begin with the expectation of Israel. Jesus is born into their hope for a Messiah.

2. The incarnation of God occurs in human history. This account is not a fairy tale; it is rooted in a specific time and place. Kings and territories and taxes and towns are named. This is the real world that has experienced a divine invasion.

3. We can see the character of God in the way Jesus comes: bringing life from death, renewing old with new, working from the bottom of the social order, assuming vulnerability among dark powers.

4. This story ignites hope among those who encounter Jesus. But it also foreshadows the reality that suffering will be the path of God in the world.

WEEK 1, DAY 4

If you have a study Bible, it may have references in a margin, a middle column, or footnotes that point to other biblical texts. You may find it helpful in understanding how the whole story of God ties together to look up some of those other scriptures from time to time.

Jesus's Birth and the Story of God

Whenever we read a biblical text, it is important to ask how the particular text we're reading relates to the rest of the Bible.

Jesus's birth, like all other stories in the Bible, has an integral place in the story of God. Specifically, we see Luke connecting the birth of Jesus to the promises of the Old Testament and its prophets. Read the following verses and record how they relate to Luke's Gospel account.

1. Genesis 3:13–15

_____

_____

_____

_____

_____

_____

_____

2. Psalm 2

_____

_____

_____

_____

_____

_____

_____

_____

3. Isaiah 7:10–17

_____

_____

_____

_____

_____

_____

_____

_____

_____

_____

4. Isaiah 9:1–7

_____

_____

_____

_____

_____

_____

_____

_____

_____

5. Isaiah 11:1–10

_____

_____

_____

_____

_____

_____

_____

_____

_____

6. Micah 5:2

Since Luke's Gospel is one of four in the New Testament, it's important to know how it aligns with and differs from the other texts of the same genre. Each of the four Gospels begins very differently. Read the following verses and note the way each writer chooses to start the story. Note the major themes, as well as any similarities or differences you find. You will also notice one non-Gospel text in this section. Read it and see what similarities you find between it and the other passages listed.

_____

_____

_____

_____

_____

7. Matthew 1:18–2:18

_____

_____

_____

_____

_____

_____

_____

8. Mark 1:1–8

_____

_____

_____

_____

_____

_____

_____

_____

_____

9. John 1:1–18

_____

_____

_____

_____

_____

_____

_____

_____

_____

_____

_____

_____

_____

_____

10. Revelation 12:1–6

_____

_____

_____

_____

_____

_____

_____

_____

_____

_____

_____

_____

_____

_____

WEEK 1, DAY 5

Luke and Our World Today

When we enter into the intriguing narrative of Luke 2:1-40, the story becomes the lens through which we see ourselves, our world, and God's action in our world today.

1. What does the story of Jesus's birth teach us?

The story of Christ's birth gives us a holy pattern to follow. As we live in community, we can be reminded that the Son of God came to this world in a way that addresses human need. Even in his birth, vulnerability and hospitality ebb and flow. As a vulnerable need rises to the surface, a hospitable act moves to meet it.

Following the above example, answer these questions about how we can understand ourselves, our world, and God's action in our world today.

2. Sometime, somewhere, the parade of wandering human need will come to your door. There will be those who need your resources, your space, your time, your help, your home. How do you typically respond when others need something from you?

3. How does it help you to remember that Jesus entered our world with great vulnerability of his own?

4. How do you attach value or worth to need?

_____

_____

_____

_____

_____

_____

_____

_____

5. Describe a time when you were in need. How did you rely on others during that time? How did others' responses affect you?

_____

_____

_____

_____

_____

_____

_____

_____

6. Where do we find vulnerability and hospitality in the stories of Simeon and Anna?

_____

_____

_____

_____

_____

_____

_____

_____

Invitation and Response

God's Word always invites a response. Think about the way the themes of vulnerability and hospitality surrounding the birth of Christ and God's incarnation speak to us today. How do they invite us to respond?

_____

_____

_____

_____

_____

_____

_____

_____

_____

_____

_____

_____

_____

_____

_____

_____

_____

_____

_____

_____

_____

_____

_____

The real world has experienced
a divine invasion.

LUKE 4:1-30

In the fourth chapter of Luke, we see the beginning of Jesus's ministry. He has been born of a virgin and baptized by John, and now it's time to get to work. This week we will explore two stories that occur right at the beginning of Jesus's ministry: his temptation by Satan in the wilderness and his conflict-ridden visit to Nazareth. As we dig into these verses, it's important to remember that Jesus defines what it means to be fully human even as he fully engages the work of his Father as the divine Son.

It's easy enough to think that Christ's divinity made his humanity more bearable. His difficult moments of temptation or ridicule by others might seem watered down to us since we ourselves encounter tough things without the benefit of divinity. But don't forget the word "fully." He was *fully* human even as he was *fully* divine. Let the word "fully" echo in your ears as we move into the beginnings of Christ's ministry.

WEEK 2, DAY 1

Listen to the story in Luke 4:1–30 by reading it aloud several times until you become familiar with its verses, words, and phrases. Enjoy the experience of imagining the story in your mind, picturing each event as it unfolds.

WEEK 2, DAY 2

LUKE 4:1–30

The Setting

In Luke 4:1–30, we have two different settings: the Judean desert and the tiny town of Nazareth.

The Judean desert is a rough place, dry and brown, littered with cliffs and caves. The hillsides are laced with dangerously narrow roads with steep inclines on one side and sharp drops on the other. On these roads, thieves with high-ground advantage could cut you off and easily surround you. There would be no way to escape. It is widely believed that the story of the Good Samaritan happened on a road like this. It's a hopeless and helpless landscape made for passing through quickly. You'd have to be out of your mind or "full of the Holy Spirit" to want to hang out in the Judean wilderness for a day, let alone forty. This is where the temptation of Jesus occurs.

The second story occurs in a more hospitable landscape—the region of Galilee. If we center ourselves on the Sea of Galilee, Nazareth is southwest by about fifteen to twenty miles. Nazareth is a hick town, a one-horse, two-bit village. It is no great honor to be from Nazareth. Yet that's where Jesus is from. And his relatives, neighbors, and all the local townsfolk have big expectations for his homecoming.

The Plot

In chapter 4, Luke is building the framework for Jesus's ministry. When Jesus is about thirty, his cousin John baptizes him, and it becomes crystal clear that Jesus is truly someone special. The Holy Spirit drops down on him like a diving dove, a voice speaks from heaven claiming him, and he starts going places—teaching, healing, and doing things only God can do. So why not start with a miracle? Luke is making sure we understand that Jesus is not going to be who anyone expects him to be. He's not in this for glory or fame. He's in ministry because we are lost and in need.

Remember that Jesus is both fully human and fully divine. That means he doesn't get an automatic pass on the testing. It doesn't come easy to him. And human hunger is no joke. Satan tempts Jesus at the moment when his humanity is the most vulnerable. The beginning of Jesus's ministry finds him in a dirty, desolate place, in a desperate human state. But remember that desperation and vulnerability are part of God's story.

It's interesting to note that in Matthew and Mark, the account of Jesus's trip to Nazareth is much shorter; they only note that the townspeople are offended by him. Luke, on the other hand, has chosen to highlight the local drama. Is Nazareth ready for the way Jesus is going to turn all expectations upside down and inside out?

Write down next to each grouping of verses the main theme(s) those verses report. Follow the pattern provided for Luke 4:1–2 and 4:3–4.

1. Luke 4:1–2

Jesus is full of the Holy Spirit and is in the wilderness. He is being tempted for for forty days. During that time, he has nothing to eat.

_____

_____

_____

_____

2. Luke 4:3–4

The devil, knowing Jesus is both fully human and hungry, tempts him to turn stone to bread. Jesus resists the temptation and quotes Scripture in response.

_____

_____

_____

3. Luke 4:5–8

_____

_____

_____

_____

_____

_____

_____

_____

_____

_____

_____

_____

_____

_____

4. Luke 4:9–13

_____

_____

_____

_____

_____

_____

_____

_____

_____

5. Luke 4:14–15

_____

_____

_____

_____

_____

_____

_____

_____

_____

_____

6. Luke 4:16–21

_____

_____

_____

_____

_____

_____

_____

_____

_____

_____

7. Luke 4:22–27

_____
_____
_____
_____
_____
_____
_____
_____
_____
_____
_____
_____
_____
_____
_____
_____

8. Luke 4:28–30

_____
_____
_____
_____
_____
_____
_____
_____
_____
_____
_____
_____
_____
_____
_____

WEEK 2, DAY 3

What's Happening in the Story?

As we notice certain circumstances in the story, we will begin to see how they are similar to or different from the realities of our world. The story will become the lens through which we see the world in which we live today. In our study today, you may encounter words and/or phrases that are unfamiliar to you. Some of the particular words and translation choices for them have been explained in more detail in the **Word Study Notes**. If you are interested in even more help or detail, you can supplement this study with a Bible dictionary or other Bible study resources.

Jot down a summary description of the world and reality that is portrayed in the following verses. Follow the pattern provided for Luke 4:14–22 and 23–30.

1. Luke 4:1–8[1, 2]

_____

_____

_____

_____

_____

_____

_____

2. Luke 4:9–13

_____

_____

_____

_____

_____

_____

WORD STUDY NOTES #1

[1] The number 40 reminds us of the time of Israel's testing in the wilderness. It is the place between the promise of deliverance and the entrance into the promised land. Israel wrestles with its identity and obedience in the wilderness. Some are faithful; others are not, and therefore never see the promised land.

[2] Satan tempts Jesus to turn stones to bread, again reminding us of the Old Testament wilderness story of the bread that came down from heaven. The difference is that Jesus can provide for himself what he needs in a way the Israelites could not. Yet his response is that his dependence is not in his own power but in the Father.

3. Luke 4:14–22

When Jesus returns to his hometown, his reputation precedes him. Local pride swells. The no-good, nowhere town of Nazareth has a bona fide hero—a God-touched, divinely energized, heaven-powered, Holy Spirited, anointed[1] prophet! Nazareth might just ride Jesus's popular coattails to a new level of honor and respectability. So when he arrives home, they honor him by asking him to read at the synagogue on the Sabbath. He reads from the scroll of the prophet Isaiah. It is the text of the suffering servant of Israel who is commissioned by God to bring good news to the poor, proclaim release to captives, recovery of sight for the blind, and liberation for the oppressed.[2] The people of Nazareth assume narrowly that they are the primary recipients of this divine favor.[3] They are amazed at the gracious words of Jesus.

4. Luke 4:23–30

The tone shifts and things quickly unravel as Jesus confronts their understanding of God's interest. Then Jesus recalls the stories of God's favor bestowed on a gentile widow in Zarephath and a Syrian military leader named Naaman. He is, in essence, announcing that their hopes are too small for God's salvation. The inaugural sermon of Jesus resets the boundaries of grace to include outsiders. Though Jacob asks for God's name, God does not reveal his identity, but instead, blesses Jacob.

WORD STUDY NOTES #3

[1] Jesus has been anointed (or christened) not by oil, as the kings of Israel in former times were, but by God's Spirit. This makes him "the anointed one," in a special sense. He is qualified to preach good news, which for Jesus means the proclamation of the kingdom of God. The very essence of Jesus's proclamation, the "kingdom of God has come," probably is indebted to this passage and to other good-news passages in Isaiah, such as 40:9 and 52:7.

[2] In verse 18, Jesus is quoting Isaiah 61:1–2. This scripture references freedom twice. But its uses are slightly different. One sense means releasing the oppressed, as in setting captives free. The other sense is close to our proclaiming freedom as forgiveness. We can therefore now view the full meaning of the word as embodied in Jesus, who came to set us free through the power of forgiveness.

[3] The "year of the Lord's favor" refers to the year of Jubilee. The Jewish understanding of time was built on seven days, with the Sabbath being the holy day of completion and rest. After seven years, a piece of ground was to be rested, or allowed to lie fallow. The year of Jubilee was the fiftieth year. It followed seven series of seven years (forty-nine years). In this year, all debt was to be forgiven and all property returned to its original family. Jubilee is God's way of recalibrating the earth, the economy, and the human condition.

Discoveries

Let's summarize our discoveries from Luke 4:1–30.

1. We often believe the Spirit will only lead us to places of affirmation and acceptance. It takes the wilderness for us to discover what lives in our hearts. In the wilderness, we discover who we are.

2. Satan quotes Scripture. Yet we know he is diametrically opposed to the work of God.

3. The things Satan tempts Jesus to do aren't necessarily bad things; rather, Satan is trying to divert Jesus from dependence on the Father, worship of the Father, and trust in the Father.

4. Jesus reminds us that there is no place he will not go to spread the good news. But the very place he might expect to be most welcome is the place that has its own agenda and is not open to his message.

WEEK 2, DAY 4

Jesus's Ministry and the Story of God

Whenever we read a biblical text, it is important to ask how the particular text we're reading relates to the rest of the Bible.

Jesus's ministry, like all other stories in the Bible, has an integral place in the story of God. In this week's passage, Jesus quotes from the Old Testament. **Read the following verses from the temptation story and record 1) how they relate to Luke's Gospel account, and 2) why you think Jesus quoted these specific verses.**

1. Deuteronomy 6:10–25

_____

_____

_____

_____

_____

_____

_____

2. Deuteronomy 8:1–10

_____

_____

_____

_____

_____

_____

_____

_____

_____

If you have a study Bible, it may have references in a margin, a middle column, or footnotes that point to other biblical texts. You may find it helpful in understanding how the whole story of God ties together to look up some of those other scriptures from time to time.

3. Isaiah 61:1–2

_____

_____

_____

_____

_____

_____

_____

4. Psalm 106

_____

_____

_____

_____

_____

_____

_____

_____

5. Psalm 91

_____

_____

_____

_____

_____

_____

_____

_____

_____

Since Luke's Gospel is one of four in the New Testament, it's important to know how it aligns with and differs from the other texts of the same genre. **Read the following verses and note the major themes, as well as any similarities or differences you find.**

6. Matthew 4:1–11

_____

_____

_____

_____

_____

_____

_____

_____

7. Matthew 13:53–58

_____

_____

_____

_____

_____

_____

_____

8. Mark 1:9–13

_____

_____

_____

_____

_____

_____

_____

WEEK 2, DAY 5

Luke and Our World Today

When we enter into the intriguing narrative of Luke 4, the story becomes the lens through which we see ourselves, our world, and God's action in our world today.

1. What does the wilderness testing tell us about Jesus and about our own temptations?

The wilderness temptations invite Jesus to do the relevant thing by turning stones to bread, to do the self-affirming thing by becoming leader of the known world, and to do the spectacular thing by leaping off the temple for the entertainment of all who need to see something exciting. When we consider these human desires—to be relevant, to rule, and to be spectacular—we find the same temptations in our own hearts. If we chase these things, we will be forever occupied by pursuits other than God—and Jesus knew that, which is why he was able to resist temptation.

Following the above example, answer these questions about how we can understand ourselves, our world, and God's action in our world today.

2. Do you generally view yourself as playing offense or defense against Satan's attack? How does the response of Jesus shape how you can face temptations?

_____

_____

_____

_____

3. What identity does Satan dangle before you? How have you responded or how are you responding?

_____

_____

_____

_____

_____

4. Jesus's visit to his hometown is a disappointment for many because he does not stoop to their agenda. How comfortable are you with disappointing people?

_____

_____

_____

_____

_____

_____

_____

_____

5. What powers and priorities do you need to say no to?

_____

_____

_____

_____

_____

_____

_____

_____

6. How does saying no at this stage in his ministry set Christ up to say yes to other things later on?

_____

_____

_____

_____

_____

_____

_____

_____

Invitation and Response

God's Word always invites a response. Think about the way the themes of temptation and reliance on God speak to us today. How does the story invite us to respond?

_____

_____

_____

_____

_____

_____

_____

_____

_____

_____

_____

_____

_____

_____

_____

_____

_____

_____

_____

_____

_____

_____

In the wilderness,
we discover who we are.

LUKE 6:17-26

Having studied Jesus's roots, birth, and social status in week 1, and his identity and mission in week 2, we now turn to the heart of Jesus's message: the kingdom of God. Prior to Luke 6, Jesus rebukes an unclean spirit, heals a feverish woman, calls disciples, cleanses a leper, heals a paralytic, and associates with a tax collector. If you are Jewish, you realize that Jesus is violating purity boundaries left and right. What people are seeing is something utterly new. Jesus has turned their ideas about purity upside down. Jesus is redefining holiness. The people whom pure and holy religious leaders would never touch become the focus of Jesus's ministry. Holiness means dirty hands of compassion and healing rather than a no-touch policy of avoidance.

The genre of these stories is called "reversal of fortune." Outsiders are in for good news—the kingdom of God has come for the likes of them. The person who expects to receive judgment and rejection due to uncleanness (illness, occupation, social status, gender, wealth, race) is surprised to receive at the hands of Jesus healing, inclusion, hospitality, forgiveness, and mercy. Their fortune has been reversed with the arrival of the kingdom of God.

WEEK 3, DAY 1

Listen to the story in Luke 6:17–26 by reading it aloud several times until you become familiar with its verses, words, and phrases. Enjoy the experience of imagining the story in your mind, picturing each event as it unfolds.

WEEK 3, DAY 2

LUKE 6:17–26

The Setting

Jesus has spent the night on the mountain praying about the selection of his disciples. You could not imagine a more diverse group of people. The competing loyalties among the twelve would rival today's political wars. As they descend from the mountain, they come to a level plain, which is why this passage is often called the Sermon on the Plain (as opposed to Matthew's Sermon on the Mount). A large crowd, some of whom have been following Jesus, has come to hear him speak. The religious system of Jesus's days denies access to certain classes and groups of people, but Jesus is here to expose how wrong that is. Those who have been corralled into exclusion by religious law are now liberated to approach God's anointed and experience the power of the Holy Spirit that flows from Jesus. He is good news to all the people. A new kingdom is coming.

The Plot

Luke records this teaching of Jesus in the middle of his public ministry, accomplishing several things for his audience. It connects the action of Jesus with the Old Testament understanding of blessing and curse. God's favor falls on some even as God's judgment falls on others. It becomes a teaching moment for why Jesus eats with sinners, heals the unclean, touches the demonized, and defiles himself among the impure. Luke connects the deeds of Jesus with the words of Jesus to give readers a fuller grasp of the essence of the new kingdom that has arrived in the person of Jesus. Jesus's teaching is more than new ideas or principles. It is *embodied* obedience to God.

Write down next to each grouping of verses the main event or theme those verses report. Follow the pattern provided for Luke 6:17–19.

1. Luke 6:17–19

Jesus is preaching to a large crowd on level ground. Some are there to listen. Others are there to be healed. Jesus has already healed some with impure spirits, and everyone wants to touch him because of the power emanating from him.

2. Luke 6:20–21

_____

_____

_____

_____

_____

_____

_____

_____

3. Luke 6:22

_____

_____

_____

_____

_____

_____

_____

_____

4. Luke 6:23

_____

_____

_____

_____

_____

_____

_____

_____

5. Luke 6:24–25

48

6. Luke 6:26

WEEK 3, DAY 3

What's Happening in the Story?

As we notice certain circumstances in the story, we will begin to see how they are similar to or different from the realities of our world. The story will become the lens through which we see the world in which we live today. In our study today, you may encounter words and/or phrases that are unfamiliar to you. Some of the particular words and translation choices for them have been explained in more detail in the **Word Study Notes**. If you are interested in even more help or detail, you can supplement this study with a Bible dictionary or other Bible study resources.

Jot down a summary description of the world and reality that is portrayed in the following verses. Follow the pattern provided for Luke 6:20-21.

1. Luke 6:17-19[1]

_____

_____

_____

_____

_____

_____

_____

_____

_____

_____

_____

_____

_____

_____

_____

_____

_____

WORD STUDY NOTES #1

[1] The Greek word that describes the kind of spirits plaguing some of the people is a word that means "unclean." The NIV uses "impure," which indicates unclean, but other translations say "evil" spirits because, at the time, anything that is unclean is also considered evil.

49

WORD STUDY NOTES #2

[1] Where Matthew uses the phrase "kingdom of heaven," Luke uses "kingdom of God." Neither refers to a place beyond the stars. It refers to the realm where God's name is hallowed and God's will done.

2. Luke 6:20-21

As he addresses his disciples, he makes eye contact with them and uses the second person ("you"). He specifically tells his followers that monetary troubles, hunger, sorrow, and all forms of hatred are impermanent. The excluded will be included. The insulted will find company with Jesus and the prophets. The rejected will be enfolded in the acceptance of God. This is the way of the kingdom.[1] In scripture, a blessing refers to words that are invested with the power to do good. On the other end of the spectrum, a curse refers to words that are invested with the power to do harm. In the Old Testament, words are deeds. They go out from the one who speaks them and cause something to happen, for good or bad. The word of God spoke creation into existence. The Word becomes flesh. Words do things. When Jesus speaks to the crowd, he is naming their situation as the focus of God's mission. The kingdom has come for the likes of them.

3. Luke 6:22-26[1, 2]

WORD STUDY NOTES #3

[1] Jesus stands in the tradition of the prophets who were persecuted for their message of social justice, covenant love, and mercy. When Jesus says "they," he could be referencing the religious leaders in Luke 5:27–6:11. And he is calling them out. As "they" did to the prophets, "they" will do to Jesus and his followers.

[2] Woe is the equivalent of the Old Testament divine curse. It is the opposite of blessing.

_____

_____

_____

_____

_____

_____

_____

_____

_____

_____

_____

_____

_____

_____

Discoveries

Let's summarize our discoveries from Luke 6:17–26.

1. The teachings of Jesus are often viewed as a code of ethics or standard of conduct. However, this assumes that Jesus is telling us what we need to become in order to be blessed. The gospel is exactly the opposite. It finds us where we are, as we are, and offers the good news that grace is flowing our way. The change we experience is that inclusion in God's life empowers us to become as human as Jesus is. And this is what holiness and purity are: being restored in the image and likeness of God.

2. The Beatitudes are not a formula for getting blessed. Instead, they are the good news that we are already blessed because the Messiah has arrived.

3. These verses are a stark contrast between what the world labels as blessing and curse and what the kingdom of God defines as blessed and cursed.

4. Religious people can really get God wrong, and when they do, they tend to punish the very prophets who understand what God is trying to do.

If you have a study Bible, it may have references in a margin, a middle column, or footnotes that point to other biblical texts. You may find it helpful in understanding how the whole story of God ties together to look up some of those other scriptures from time to time.

The Kingdom of God and the Story of God

Whenever we read a biblical text, it is important to ask how the particular text we're reading relates to the rest of the Bible. References to the kingdom of God can be found all throughout the Bible.

In the space provided, write a short summary of how the kingdom is described and how Jesus fulfills this prophetic hope.

1. Psalm 94

_____

_____

_____

_____

_____

_____

2. Psalm 95

_____

_____

_____

_____

_____

_____

3. Isaiah 11:1–9

_____

_____

_____

_____

_____

_____

4. Isaiah 35

_____

_____

_____

_____

_____

_____

_____

_____

_____

5. Micah 6:8

_____

_____

_____

_____

_____

_____

_____

_____

_____

Luke is filled with references to the kingdom of God. Read the following texts and write a short summary of what these passages tell us about the kingdom of God.

6. Luke 8:1–15

_____

_____

_____

_____

_____

_____

_____

_____

7. Luke 11:1–5

_____
_____
_____
_____
_____
_____
_____
_____

8. Luke 12:22–34

_____
_____
_____
_____
_____
_____
_____
_____

9. Luke 13:18–21

_____
_____
_____
_____
_____
_____
_____
_____
_____

WEEK 3, DAY 5

Luke and Our World Today

When we enter into the intriguing narrative of Luke 6, the story becomes the lens through which we see ourselves, our world, and God's action in our world today.

1. If someone were to ask, "What is the kingdom of God?" what would an appropriate answer be?

Some say it is heaven, where we will go after we die. Some say it is the ultimate place of safety and refuge that we escape to. Some say it is the church, where people serve God. Some say it is the future that will dawn on us when Jesus returns. So what is it? Quite simply, it is the place where God's will is done.

Following the above example, answer these questions about how we can understand ourselves, our world, and God's action in our world today.

2. What does it mean when we pray, "Your kingdom come"?

3. Whom do you know who feels excluded from God but, according to our text, would actually be offered blessing?

4. Whom do you know (perhaps yourself?) who believes they are an insider with God but might actually stand under judgment?

_____

_____

_____

_____

_____

_____

_____

_____

5. Do your words and actions tend to bless or curse the people you do life with?

_____

_____

_____

_____

_____

_____

_____

_____

Invitation and Response

God's Word always invites a response. Imagine yourself among the crowd on the plain for Jesus's sermon. He lifts his eyes, looks at you, and speaks directly to you. What does Luke 6:17–26 mean in your life? What does the kingdom of God mean in your life? How does the story invite you to respond?

_____

_____

_____

_____

_____

The gospel finds us where we are, as we are, and offers the good news that grace is flowing our way.

LUKE 6:27-49

In this week's text, we continue our study of the Sermon on the Plain with some of the most well-known teachings of Jesus. Jesus's audience is a mixture of outcasts, religious rulers, and newly minted disciples. Each group hears these words from a different perspective. What is good news to some is bad news to others. And the faint drumbeat of coming rejection is growing stronger as Jesus speaks about being hated, reviled, and having enemies.

WEEK 4, DAY 1

Listen to the story in Luke 6:27–49 by reading it aloud several times until you become familiar with its verses, words, and phrases. Enjoy the experience of imagining the story in your mind, picturing each event as it unfolds.

WEEK 4, DAY 2

LUKE 6:27-49

The Setting

We are at the foot of the mountain where Jesus prayed and called disciples to follow him. We are facing the crowds that have gathered in hopes of healing and deliverance from evil spirits and demons. We are confronted by the scowl of religious leaders who are bothered that the ancient purity laws of the Jews are being violated by this young rabbi. We are standing alongside rookie disciples who have not begun to understand the depth of dark resistance to the words and deeds of the carpenter from Nazareth. Remember that these teachings are being delivered in gentile territory, which provides important context for what Jesus is saying.

The Plot

The simplicity of Jesus's instructions allows us to summarize his teaching in short, direct phrases that most people would recognize. *Turn the other cheek. Remove the log from your own eye. Bear fruit. Build your house upon the rock.* As you study these popular lessons for the first time or the hundredth, pay attention to why Jesus used specific metaphors, how they have endured over thousands of years, and why they continue to resonate today.

This week's passage immediately follows the reversal-of-fortune sermon that incorporates the Beatitudes, so the setting hasn't changed. Jesus has just turned the expected order on its head. Now, he proceeds to teach the people how to live and behave in the new kingdom. And things go from weird to weirder. He teaches them to do the opposite of what might be expected. **Write down next to each grouping of verses the main event or theme those verses report. Follow the pattern provided for Luke 6:27–31.**

1. Luke 6:27–31

Jesus is talking about human responses to wrong that are the exact opposite of what is

instinctive. Give love in exchange for hate, speak blessing in return for cursing, offer prayer

in exchange for abuse, offer a defenseless cheek in exchange for a slap, gift the thief who

stole your cloak with your shirt as well, give beggars whatever you have, when robbed

don't demand your possession back.

2. Luke 6:32–34

_____

_____

_____

_____

_____

_____

3. Luke 6:35–36

_____

_____

_____

_____

_____

_____

4. Luke 6:37–38

_____

_____

_____

_____

_____

_____

5. Luke 6:39–40

_____

_____

_____

_____

_____

6. Luke 6:41–42

7. Luke 6:43–45

8. Luke 6:46–49

WEEK 4, DAY 3

What's Happening in the Story?

As we notice certain circumstances in the story, we will begin to see how they are similar to or different from the realities of our world. The story will become the lens through which we see the world in which we live today. In our study today, you may encounter words and/or phrases that are unfamiliar to you. Some of the particular words and translation choices for them have been explained in more detail in the **Word Study Notes**. If you are interested in even more help or detail, you can supplement this study with a Bible dictionary or other Bible study resources.

Jot down a summary description of the world and reality that is portrayed in the following verses. Follow the pattern provided for Luke 6:43–45.

1. Luke 6:27–31

_____

_____

_____

_____

_____

_____

Luke 6:32–36[1]

_____

_____

_____

_____

_____

_____

WORD STUDY NOTES #2

[1] Compare verse 36 to its companion, Matthew 5:48. Matthew concludes with perfection while Luke chooses mercy. Both texts indicate that loving our enemies has an element of God's holy perfection and God's mercy.

3. Luke 6:37–42 [1,2]

_____

_____

_____

_____

_____

_____

_____

_____

4. Luke 6:43–45

The essence of a tree comes out in its fruit, even as the essence of the heart comes out in our words and deeds.[1] Sooner or later, the real person shows up, for good or evil. Rather than judging, we must practice patience. Patience allows people time to reveal who they really are. They history of a person does not lie. And the only thing that can change the trajectory of history is an encounter with Jesus, the removal of a log in the eye, the fullness of mercy in the heart.

5. Luke 6:46–49 [1]

_____

_____

_____

_____

_____

_____

_____

_____

Discoveries

Let's summarize our discoveries from Luke 6:27–49.

1. Christian perfection is the call to reflect the God who created us. We are to love as God loves and show mercy as God shows mercy. In our own power, we are incapable of this, but the gift of the Spirit brings the presence and power of Jesus to the core of our being. God empowers the life that the kingdom calls for.

2. The ethic of the kingdom is countercultural. To follow the way of Jesus is to step out of the current of the world and into the current of God's kingdom river.

3. Humans have the capacity to stand in the way of needy people by judging them, shaming them, and causing them to believe that God despises them. This makes God angry.

4. Our standard of behavior is never to compare ourselves with others but to seek restoration in likeness to Jesus.

WEEK 4, DAY 4

If you have a study
Bible, it may have
references in a
margin, a middle
column, or footnotes
that point to other
biblical texts. You
may find it helpful
in understanding
how the whole
story of God ties
together to look up
some of those other
scriptures from time
to time.

The Teachings of Jesus and the Story of God

Whenever we read a biblical text, it is important to ask how the particular text we're reading relates to the rest of the Bible.

Jesus's sermons, like all other stories in the Bible, have an integral place in the story of God. The Old Testament contains several verses where we can learn more about what Jesus commands his followers. **In the space provided, write a short summary of how this theme is seen in each passage.**

1. Deuteronomy 15:1–11

_____

_____

_____

_____

_____

_____

_____

2. Proverbs 21:25–26

_____

_____

_____

_____

_____

_____

_____

_____

3. Proverbs 25:21–22

_____

_____

_____

_____

_____

_____

_____

_____

_____

4. Jeremiah 31:31–34

_____

_____

_____

_____

_____

_____

We also see references to the teachings of Jesus in other places in the New Testament. **In the space given below, write a short summary of how these themes connect with Luke 6.**

5. Matthew 23:1–36

_____

_____

_____

_____

_____

_____

_____

_____

_____

_____

6. Luke 3:10–14

_____
_____
_____
_____
_____
_____
_____
_____
_____
_____
_____
_____
_____
_____
_____

7. 1 Peter 2:18–25

_____
_____
_____
_____
_____
_____
_____
_____
_____
_____
_____
_____
_____
_____
_____
_____

WEEK 4, DAY 5

Luke and Our World Today

When we enter the Gospel of Luke, the story becomes the lens through which we see ourselves, our world, and God's action in our world today.

1. What do the teachings of Jesus in Luke's Gospel say to us about ourselves, our world, and God's action in our world today?

The passage this week tells us quite specifically how to respond in ways that reflect the

kingdom of God. These words call us to Christlikeness. To be a Christian is to be like Jesus, to

experience his death and resurrection, and to be filled with his empowering Spirit. Luke

invites us to respond to Jesus by repenting of our worldly ways, forsaking our sin, ceasing our

judgment of others, and coming to God just as we are. Until we respond in these ways, we are

closed to the gifts of the kingdom. We hinder the salvation that seeks us.

Following the above example, answer these questions about how we can understand ourselves, our world, and God's action in our world today.

2. What does it look like to tangibly love our enemies?

_____

_____

_____

_____

_____

3. Why are humans most blind to their own sins? How can we remedy that?

_____

_____

_____

_____

_____

_____

4. Think about the metaphor of bearing fruit and how it relates to the passage of time and seasons in the natural world. How might this shed more light on why Jesus used this specific example?

_____

_____

_____

_____

_____

_____

Invitation and Response

God's Word always invites a response. Think about the way the themes from Jesus's teachings speak to us today. How do they invite us to respond?

It is important in our walk with God that we hear the teachings of Jesus as snapshots of the
life that God empowers, not pre-conditions for earning salvation. The only way to love our enemy,
show mercy, bear fruit, stop judging, and build our house on the rock is to respond to the
gracious offer embedded in the good news of the kingdom.

What is your evaluation of yourself based on Luke 6:27–49?

_____

_____

_____

_____

_____

_____

_____

_____

_____

_____

_____

God empowers
the life that God's
kingdom calls for.

LUKE 8:22-39

This week we move from studying Jesus the public speaker to learning about Jesus the activist. Through the power given to him by God, he is actively setting right things that are wrong, healing the sick, freeing the imprisoned, gifting peace to those who are afraid, and restoring life to the dead.

The miracles in this passage contrast in a couple ways. We have the ultimate insiders, Jesus's Jewish disciples, and the ultimate outsider, a demon-possessed gentile. The first miracle is performed for the benefit of those whom we would expect to have the most faith. After all, the disciples are the team Christ has chosen to follow him and continue his work after he is gone. The beneficiary of the second miracle is about as far on the other side of the spectrum as you can get—a man possessed by many demons and ostracized from society in every way. Yet, while the faith of the disciples is called into question, the demon-possessed man knows exactly who Jesus is and what power Jesus has. Once again, we see an invitation and a response, and vulnerability that is greeted with hospitality.

WEEK 5, DAY 1

Listen to the story in Luke 8:22–39 by reading it aloud several times until you become familiar with its verses, words, and phrases. Enjoy the experience of imagining the story in your mind, picturing each event as it unfolds.

WEEK 5, DAY 2

LUKE 8:22-39

The Setting

These stories take place on and near what is often called the Sea of Galilee, but it is actually more of a large lake. The stories are set in gentile territory, north of Jerusalem, as Jesus continues to minister to outsiders. We get the feeling that it is a typical day as Jesus says, "Let's go over to the other side of the lake" (v. 22). But the disciples are about to see Jesus's power displayed in new and mighty ways.

The Plot

This passage chronicles two miracles, both of which serve to expand the territory of Jesus's good news and power. In the first scene, Jesus calms a storm that threatens the boat he and his followers are traveling in. In the second, he heals and frees a man who has long been possessed by many demons. As Jesus moves from town to town, word of his power continues to spread.

These are two of a series of four miracles found also in Matthew and Mark: calming the storm, performing an exorcism, healing a bleeding woman, and raising a girl from the dead. These miracles are closely followed by the sending of the disciples.

Write down next to each grouping of verses the main event or theme those verses report. Follow the pattern provided for Luke 8:22–23

1. Luke 8:22–23

Jesus and his disciples have set out to minister and are traveling across a lake. Jesus has fallen asleep when a storm rolls in. The disciples are afraid for their lives.

_____

_____

2. Luke 8:24

_____

_____

_____

_____

_____

3. Luke 8:25

_____
_____
_____
_____
_____
_____

4. Luke 8:26–27

_____
_____
_____
_____
_____
_____

5. Luke 8:28–29

_____
_____
_____
_____
_____
_____

6. Luke 8:30–31

_____
_____
_____
_____
_____
_____

7. Luke 8:32–33

_____

_____

_____

_____

_____

_____

_____

8. Luke 8:34–36

_____

_____

_____

_____

_____

_____

_____

9. Luke 8:37–39

_____

_____

_____

_____

_____

_____

_____

WEEK 5, DAY 3

What's Happening in the Story?

As we notice certain circumstances in the story, we will begin to see how they are similar to or different from the realities of our world. The story will become the lens through which we see the world in which we live today. In our study today, you may encounter words and/or phrases that are unfamiliar to you. Some of the particular words and translation choices for them have been explained in more detail in the **Word Study Notes**. If you are interested in even more help or detail, you can supplement this study with a Bible dictionary or other Bible study resources.

Jot down a summary description of the world and reality that is portrayed in the following verses. Follow the pattern provided for Luke 8:26–27, 30–31, and 37–39.

1. Luke 8:22–25[1]

_____

_____

_____

_____

_____

_____

_____

_____

WORD STUDY NOTES #1

[1] They have traveling companions who have been "cured of evil spirits and diseases" (Luke 8:2). But for some reason, Jesus's power in this situation surprises his followers. Some believe it is because he is commanding the waters, which in ancient times are generally seen as chaotic, and under the reign of dark forces. Others believe it is because he is performing miracles outside of Jewish territory.

2. Luke 8:26–27

The character in this story has Jewish uncleanness and impurity written all over him: demons, tombs, dead people, nakedness, living in the wild. In addition, the scene unfolds in gentile territory, and it has pigs—the ultimate unclean animal. This man, like the storm Jesus just quelled, cannot be controlled by humans. Everyone knows they are facing something beyond human control.

3. Luke 8:28-29

_____
_____
_____
_____
_____
_____
_____
_____
_____
_____
_____
_____
_____
_____
_____
_____

WORD STUDY NOTES #4

[1] A legion is the name for the Roman army's largest unit. A typical legion has between three thousand and six thousand soldiers.

[2] Scholars do not agree on what "abyss" refers to. It could be a reference to the chaotic waters, indicating that is where the demons came from. It could be a reference to a spirit underworld or the world of the dead. Or it could be a reference to a place where demons and evil spirits are judged.

4. Luke 8:30-31

Jesus interacts with the troubled man, asking his name. For a man who has been literally stripped of everything else—his home, his town, his friends, his clothes, and his sanity—his name might be all that is left of his humanity. But even his name is a reflection of the dark spirits that control him. "Legion," he replies—because to try to name all the dark spirits inside him would take too long.[1] He has become an apartment complex for demons, and they've gladly taken up residence. The demons are quite happy where they are, tormenting this man, and they also recognize Jesus for who he is, so they beg him not to send them "into the Abyss."[2]

5. Luke 8:32-36[1]

_____

_____

_____

_____

_____

_____

_____

_____

_____

_____

_____

_____

_____

_____

_____

_____

6. Luke 8:37-39

The reaction of the townspeople is interesting. They spread the word, just as Luke is doing by writing the Gospel. People come to see the evidence and discover the wild man sitting at Jesus's feet, clothed and calm. They are afraid.[1] Their fear is so great that they ask Jesus to leave, so he leaves. But the healed man begs to follow. This is the response of the one who has been delivered from darkness—to follow. Jesus recognizes that kingdom witness is needed in the man's hometown. By staying, he can give this city a daily reminder of the power of God over evil. Every time the people see the man, they will not be able to help but recall the day that the God of power stood in their cemetery and gave a man back his life.

WORD STUDY NOTES #5

[1] The swine in the story are a rare occurrence in the stories about Jesus. The Jews considered swine an unclean animal, and did not raise them. Only in this story, where Jesus goes to gentile territory, do we find pigs.

WORD STUDY NOTES #6

[1] Note that the response of the townspeople to the healing of the demoniac is the same as the response of the disciples to the taming of the storm: they are afraid. Neither the Jewish disciples nor the gentiles have a category for one who has the power to tame a sea storm or a storm in the body of a human. But it's interesting that the same response—fear—leads to opposite reactions. The disciples' fear leads to their continuing to follow Jesus, but the gentiles do not respond with the same open curiosity. They are threatened by a power that is beyond their own.

Discoveries

Let's summarize our discoveries from Luke 8:22–39.

1. We returned this week to the vulnerable-hospitable loop that is so prevalent in Luke. Jesus models for his followers a pattern of encountering vulnerability and responding with hospitality.

2. Jesus crosses boundaries not for the sake of crossing boundaries or for the purpose of angering people but for the sake of love.

3. Jesus's power (and, by extension, God's power) is incomprehensible — and as limitless as God's love. It is not restrained by anything or anyone.

WEEK 5, DAY 4

The Miracles of Jesus and the Story of God

Whenever we read a biblical text, it is important to ask how the particular text we're reading relates to the rest of the Bible. Jesus's miracles like all other stories in the Bible, have an integral place in the story of God.

Today we will place the miracles of Luke 8 in the broader context of the Old Testament understanding of God. As you follow the suggested texts, record your insights regarding the way this theme connects with Luke 8.

1. Genesis 1:1–10

_____

_____

_____

_____

_____

2. Genesis 6:5–22

_____

_____

_____

_____

_____

3. Psalm 29

_____

_____

_____

_____

_____

If you have a study Bible, it may have references in a margin, a middle column, or footnotes that point to other biblical texts. You may find it helpful in understanding how the whole story of God ties together to look up some of those other scriptures from time to time.

We also see the miracles of Jesus referenced many places in the New Testament. In the space provided, write a short summary of how the following passages relate to our passage this week.

4. Revelation 4:6

_____
_____
_____
_____
_____
_____
_____
_____

5. Revelation 12:18–13:4

_____
_____
_____
_____
_____
_____
_____

6. Revelation 21:1

_____
_____
_____
_____
_____
_____
_____
_____
_____

WEEK 5, DAY 5

Luke and Our World Today

When we enter into the Gospel of Luke, the story becomes the lens through which we see ourselves, our world, and God's action in our world today..

1. What do these miracles of Jesus say to us about ourselves, our world, and God's action in our world today?

It is no stretch of imagination to see that the chaotic storm that threatens the disciples on the Sea of Galilee is paralleled in the man who lives among the tombs. Chaos has taken up residence in him. It is one thing to be threatened by the external chaos of the world. It is quite another to have chaos living in us and calling us by its own name. This passage reminds us that there is no chaos that Jesus cannot calm.

Following the above example, answer these questions about how we can understand ourselves, our world, and God's action in our world today.

2. Where do you observe chaos in our world today? What forms does it take? How is it like a sea of untamed darkness??

_____

_____

_____

_____

_____

3. During the course of your life, what things have sin and darkness robbed you of that you've seen Jesus restore? Name a time when God tamed the storm in your life.

_____

_____

_____

_____

_____

_____

_____

4. Why are the townspeople afraid of Jesus? What is it about Jesus that is more dangerous than a demon-possessed man?

_____

_____

_____

_____

_____

_____

_____

_____

_____

_____

_____

_____

Invitation and Response

God's Word always invites a response. Think about the way the themes of Jesus's power and the way Jesus responds to chaos speak to us today. How does the story invite us to respond?

_____

_____

_____

_____

_____

_____

_____

_____

_____

_____

_____

_____

_____

Jesus models fr his followers a
pattern of encountering vulnerability
and responding with hospitality.

LUKE 10:25-37

This week's passage is about a character who was etched into humanity's collective memory forever with two labels: "good" and "Samaritan." These words are markers, identifiers, descriptors. We use labels often in today's world, just as labels were used often in Jesus's world. Jesus himself was not exempt from human labels: *Friend of sinners. Blasphemer. King of the Jews. Son of God. Messiah. Christ. Healer. Teacher. Friend.*

Labels can be used to speak blessing or curse into the lives of others. We use them to shape our own identities and the identities of others. In the parable this week, Jesus has a lot to say about labels. He's not a fan of the kinds of labels that allow us to dismiss others or labels that seem to excuse us from exercising generous hospitality.

WEEK 6, DAY 1

Listen to the story in Luke 10:25–37 by reading it aloud several times until you become familiar with its verses, words, and phrases. Enjoy the experience of imagining the story in your mind, picturing each event as it unfolds.

The Setting

We have already studied some of the teachings of Jesus in the Gospel of Luke. Another way Jesus taught is through parables. Reading or hearing a parable requires that we recognize the context into which the story fits. Luke is not telling us that this event literally happened to someone Jesus knew. He is telling us that an encounter with a young scribe prompted Jesus to tell this (probably fictional) story. The story is understandable to Jesus's audience because it is constructed from the reality of the road to Jericho, the reality of thieves, and the reality of existing prejudices toward certain groups.

The story of the Good Samaritan takes place on the road between Jerusalem and Jericho. It's not a nice road—not one you'd take the family on for a scenic journey. It's known to be frequented by miscreants and criminals. And the physical makeup of the road contributes to its danger. The journey spans a distance of about seventeen miles and drops in altitude nearly half a mile over that stretch. Because the road is sandwiched between hills, it provides plenty of tactical advantages to those wanting to take advantage of travelers.

The Plot

The story begins with "an expert in the law" standing up to try to trick Jesus. We see this pattern often in the Gospels. "Expert in the law" likely does not mean a lawyer in today's sense of the word, but an expert in Jewish law—that is, Torah. This "expert in the law" is, therefore, a Jewish religious leader—one who probably feels threatened by Jesus's popularity and his boundary-crossing behaviors, hence why he wants to test Jesus. He might be hoping to catch Jesus being "wrong" about a technical matter of the law. Or he could just be hoping for a good debate. The parable Jesus tells in this context is one that expertly navigates the expert's interrogation. Like the typical lawyers we are familiar with today, this expert in the law is looking for a loophole. What he finds instead is an articulation of Jesus's mission in the world.

Write down next to each grouping of verses the main event or theme those verses report. Follow the pattern given provided for Luke 10:25–26 and 27–29.

1. Luke 10:25–26

Luke tells us that an expert in the law asks Jesus a question. We know this label means that he understands the Old Testament law and tradition. He is the ultimate insider as a member of God's covenanted people. Luke wants us to know that he is testing Jesus. Jesus behaves like a good rabbi in response to his question—by answering with a question.

2. Luke 10:27–29

The expert in the law answers his own question about what qualifies one to inherit eternal life. And Jesus affirms his answer as scripturally correct. The story should end here. But it doesn't. Luke again reveals the scribe's motive by showing us that he is looking for a loophole in asking Jesus to define who his neighbor is.

3. Luke 10:30

4. Luke 10:31–32

_____
_____
_____
_____
_____
_____
_____
_____
_____

5. Luke 10:33–35

_____
_____
_____
_____
_____
_____
_____
_____

6. Luke 10:36–37

_____
_____
_____
_____
_____
_____
_____
_____

WEEK 6, DAY 3

What's Happening in the Story?

As we notice certain circumstances in the story, we will begin to see how they are similar to or different from the realities of our world. The story will become the lens through which we see the world in which we live today. In our study today, you may encounter words and/or phrases that are unfamiliar to you. Some of the particular words and translation choices for them have been explained in more detail in the **Word Study Notes**. If you are interested in even more help or detail, you can supplement this study with a Bible dictionary or other Bible study resources.

Jot down a summary description of the world and reality that is portrayed in the following verses. Follow the pattern provided for Luke 10:30, 33, and 34–35.

1. Luke 10:25–27[1]

_____

_____

_____

_____

_____

_____

_____

_____

_____

_____

_____

_____

_____

WORD STUDY NOTES #1

[1] In Jewish tradition, debate is common, expected, and welcome. It doesn't always mean those who begin debates have malicious motives. Jesus interprets the Torah differently than anyone they have previously encountered, so it makes sense that many Torah experts want to debate or challenge him. But Luke and other Gospel writers make clear that some of those who pose questions to Jesus do have dishonest intentions.

[1] The expert in the law has asked Jesus to define "neighbor" so he can "justify himself." The word translated "justify" is a math or business term that we would use today in reference to balancing the checkbook or certifying inventory. It means that the expected standard is met.

[2] The question about who our neighbors are directly follows the passage that opens Luke 10, where Jesus has sent out seventy-two disciples to minister in the darkness of the world in neighboring communities and towns. The juxtaposition could indicate that this man's understanding of neighbor is too narrow, only extending to loving the people who belong to his family, his temple, his clan.

2. Luke 10:28–29 [1,2]

_____

_____

_____

_____

_____

_____

_____

_____

3. Luke 10:30

In the parable, the robbed and beaten man in the ditch becomes a literary foil. He has no lines. We learn things about other characters as they react to him. It is interesting that we get no description of him. We do not know if he is a Jew or gentile, local or foreign, moral or a sinner. We only know his present condition—needy, vulnerable, and unable to help himself.

4. Luke 10:31–32

_____

_____

_____

_____

_____

_____

_____

_____

_____

5. Luke 10:33

If there is a moment of shock in the parable, it is the introduction of the Samaritan.[1] This man becomes the hero of the story. The scribe is swallowing hard to stomach that such an unclean person would be the model of neighbor love.

6. Luke 10:34-35

In the parable, the robbed and beaten man in the ditch becomes a literary foil. He has no lines. We learn things about other characters as they react to him. It is interesting that we get no description of him. We do not know if he is a Jew or gentile, local or foreign, moral or a sinner. We only know his present condition—needy, vulnerable, and unable to help himself.

7. Luke 10:36-37[1]

_____

_____

_____

_____

_____

_____

_____

_____

_____

_____

_____

_____

_____

_____

_____

_____

WORD STUDY NOTES #5

[1] The Samaritans are viewed by the Israelites as impure half-breeds whose ancestors violated the covenant and went rogue on orthodoxy. That's why it is surprising and ironic that a Samaritan becomes the hero of Jesus's story, displaying godly love when others who are expected to act in love do not.

WORD STUDY NOTES #7

[1] Once again, we hear the term "mercy" used to describe someone who demonstrates a likeness to God. See Luke 1:50; 1:72; 6:36.

Discoveries

Let's summarize our discoveries from Luke 10:25–37.

1. Purity boundaries tell Jewish leaders whom they can and cannot touch. The expert in the law's real question is not "who is my neighbor?" but "just how far does the welcome of God's kingdom extend?"

2. Religion that justifies ignoring human need is not the religion of Jesus.

3. Sometimes we see more compassion from so-called sinners than from front–pew believers.

4. It is possible to (mis)use Scripture in a way that excuses us from obedience to God and love of neighbor.

5. It is always easier to pass judgment and label others than it is to help them.

WEEK 6, DAY 4

The Good Samaritan and the Story of God

Whenever we read a biblical text, it is important to ask how the text we are reading relates to the rest of the Bible.

The parables told by Jesus have an integral place in the story of God. **In the space provided, write a short summary of how the following verses relate to the passage we are studying this week.**

1. Leviticus 19:33–34

_____

_____

_____

_____

_____

_____

2. Deuteronomy 6:1–9

_____

_____

_____

_____

_____

_____

3. Deuteronomy 10:12–22

_____

_____

_____

_____

_____

_____

If you have a study Bible, it may have references in a margin, a middle column, or footnotes that point to other biblical texts. You may find it helpful in understanding how the whole story of God ties together to look up some of those other scriptures from time to time.

95

4. Luke 9:51–56

_____
_____
_____
_____
_____
_____
_____
_____
_____

5. Acts 2:42–47

_____
_____
_____
_____
_____
_____
_____
_____
_____

6. Romans 15:1–13

_____
_____
_____
_____
_____
_____
_____
_____
_____

WEEK 6, DAY 5

Luke and Our World Today

When we enter into the intriguing narrative of Luke 10:25-37, the story becomes the lens through which we see ourselves, our world, and God's action in our world today.

1. What does the parable of the Good Samaritan say to us about ourselves, our world, and God's action in our world today?

This parable has so ingrained itself in our culture that the phrase "Good Samaritan" is used to speak of human kindness and mercy wherever it is found. The life of Jesus is the clearest picture we will ever see of what the Old Testament law required and what the prophets imagined. It is not the law that has misled the scribe. The law depicts what is possible for the one who lives in Christ, empowered by the Spirit. The problem here is that the scribe has interpreted the law through the lens of his own bias.

Following the above example, answer these questions about how we can understand ourselves, our world, and God's action in our world today.

2. The key words in Deuteronomy and Leviticus are "remember that you were strangers." What memory do you have that motivates you to be hospitable and to show mercy to the helpless?

_____

_____

_____

_____

3. Who are the people who have been beaten and abandoned by our culture, who do not have anyone who views them as neighbor? What would it look like for you to be their neighbor?

_____

_____

_____

_____

4. How do we use labels to keep us from interacting with certain people today?

_____

_____

_____

_____

_____

_____

5. Have you ever been helped by a Good Samaritan? How did that encounter change you?

_____

_____

_____

_____

_____

_____

Invitation and Response

God's Word always invites a response. Think about the way the themes of abandonment and unexpected or radical hospitality speak to us today. How does the story invite us to respond?

_____

_____

_____

_____

_____

_____

_____

_____

_____

Religion that justifies
ignoring human
need is not the
religion of Jesus.

LUKE 24:13-35

We've studied the Gospel of Luke from theological and literary perspectives, paying attention to setting and plot and language. Luke's story of Jesus places him in the middle of humanity. He offers life and receives death. He extends hospitable space and receives cold rejection. He speaks truth and is crucified under the guise of blasphemy. The only place the world is willing to house Jesus is in a borrowed tomb. The resurrection is God's way of confirming that Jesus is Messiah, that his words are true, that his love is pure, and that his mercy is transforming. Resurrection doesn't end when Jesus steps out of the tomb or when he ascends into heaven. It's still at work now, today, in the very moment you are reading this. May the words you read in Luke's Gospel come alive to you like never before. May you celebrate the resurrection with both stark reality and fullness of joy. Hear the themes of invitation and response, vulnerability and hospitality one final time in this beautiful chapter.

WEEK 7, DAY 1

Listen to the story in Luke 24:13–35 by reading it aloud several times until you become familiar with its verses, words, and phrases. Enjoy the experience of imagining the story in your mind, picturing each event as it unfolds.

WEEK 7, DAY 2

LUKE 24:13–35

The Setting

Luke 24 has multiple settings, not least of which include a graveside, a country road, and a dinner table. Of course, we know that the graveside hosts the famous empty tomb, where Jesus's body was not found because he had risen. The second setting is that of a country road that runs the seven-mile, east-west stretch between the towns of Emmaus and Jerusalem. It serves as the scene for an important conversation between the resurrected Messiah and two of his followers. This story then transitions to the scene of a dinner table after Cleopas opens his home to Jesus. This setting is familiar throughout the story of Christ: a home opened in warm hospitality, a meal graciously shared and received. This story will be the focus of our study this week.

The Plot

The settings of Luke 24 are intimately tied to the plot in powerful ways. Recall how the kingdom of God is all about reversal of fortunes. The empty tomb represents a final reversal. A graveyard hasn't ever been a place people emerge from yelling good news at breakneck speed—until now. This is a plot twist like none other. Recall also Christ's birth, and how he came into the world in a place made available to his family through the hospitality of others. It should not surprise us that the first place Jesus is recognized after his resurrection is in a home that is opened to him through hospitality. **In the space provided, write down next to each grouping of verses the main theme those verses report. Follow the pattern provided for Luke 24:15–16.**

1. Luke 24:13–14

_____

_____

_____

_____

2. Luke 24:15–16

The text tells us very carefully that "they were kept from recognizing him." We are not told

uwho or what keeps them from recognizing him. Jesus comes alongside and asks what they are

discussing. The best they can do is stand still, looking sad.

3. Luke 24:17–21

4. Luke 24:22–24

5. Luke 24:25–29

6. Luke 24:30–32

_____
_____
_____
_____
_____
_____
_____
_____
_____
_____
_____
_____
_____
_____

7. Luke 24:33–35

_____
_____
_____
_____
_____
_____
_____
_____
_____
_____
_____
_____
_____

WEEK 7, DAY 3

What's Happening in the Story?

As we notice certain circumstances in the story, we will begin to see how they are similar to or different from the realities of our world. The story will become the lens through which we see the world in which we live today. In our study today, you may encounter words and/or phrases that are unfamiliar to you. Some of the particular words and translation choices for them have been explained in more detail in the **Word Study Notes**. If you are interested in even more help or detail, you can supplement this study with a Bible dictionary or other Bible study resources.

1. Luke 24:13-17

_____

_____

_____

_____

_____

_____

_____

WORD STUDY NOTES #2

[1] Many believe that these two are husband and wife. If you think about them inviting Jesus in at the end of the walk, setting the table, and offering a guest room, it makes sense that they could be husband and wife.

[2] The brief description of Jesus as "a prophet, powerful in word and deed before God and all the people" is a classic Lukan understanding of Jesus as the fulfillment of the Old Testament role of prophet.

2. Luke 24:18-19[1, 2]

_____

_____

_____

_____

_____

_____

_____

_____

3. Luke 24:20-27[1]

The road conversation is intriguing. They explain to Jesus what happened to Jesus, as if he does not know. They talk about their former hopes. Jesus listens. And when he does start talking, he gives them a biblical review of the law and the prophets.[2] These two have it all scripted. Messiah comes, Messiah is enthroned, Messiah reigns. That's how the story goes. This stranger on the road offers a different plotline: Messiah comes, Messiah is rejected, Messiah is crucified, Messiah is dead and buried, Messiah is raised.

4. Luke 24:28-32[1, 2]

_____

_____

_____

_____

_____

_____

5. Luke 24:33-35

_____

_____

_____

_____

_____

_____

_____

_____

_____

_____

_____

WORD STUDY NOTES #3

[1] Note the use of Luke's phrase "the women" in verses 22-24. Given the fact that the testimony of a woman is not reliable in court in this culture, this is a radical affirmation of the role that women played in bearing testimony to the risen Jesus.

[2] References to "the law and the prophets" are often used to speak of the full weight of the hopes of Israel. Together, they speak of the covenant path of obedience to the law and the prophetic insistence that this way of life be applied in every historical situation in which Israel finds itself.

WORD STUDY NOTES #4

[1] Note the significance of what is happening here. The resurrected Jesus is breaking bread and offering it to his hosts.

[2] When Jesus breaks the bread, their eyes are opened. Just as carefully as the text tells us they were kept from recognizing him, it tells us that their eyes were opened. The use of passive voice is intentional. These two are not acting—they are being acted upon. Forces beyond them are doing things to their eyes that they do not control.

105

Discoveries

Let's summarize our discoveries from Luke 24:13–35.

1. The resurrection cannot be explained in a way that makes sense. And the people around the resurrection respond to it with fear and amazement and pure, unfiltered emotions. That's all God expects from us still: that we experience the resurrection with fear and amazement and unfiltered human emotions.

2. Women are the first eyewitnesses of the resurrection light. They were the first to be entrusted with the news of the resurrection—the first preachers of the gospel of Christ.

3. The risen Lord is recognized by his hands and feet. Our world mostly identifies people by their faces—but Jesus shows them his hands to prove his identity. These are hands that held children, healed diseases, cast out demons, broke bread, pressed mud into blind eyes, stilled storms, pointed at fig trees, and split wide open when pierced by spikes. He also shows them his feet. These are the same feet that walked on water, carried good news to the unworthy, moved among the last and the least, were doused with perfume, bore the weight of a cross, and broke and bled under the nail driven through them. And they knew it was him.

WEEK 7, DAY 4

The Resurrection of Jesus and the Story of God

Whenever we read a biblical text, it is important to ask how the particular text we're reading relates to the rest of the Bible.

In the Old Testament we see a lot about suffering but not a robust resurrection hope. But when we read backwards into the stories of Israel, we find that resurrection is embedded in the character of God. **In the space provided, write a short summary of how the following scriptures from both the Old and New Testaments relate to the theme of resurrection.**

1. Psalm 22

_____

_____

_____

_____

_____

_____

_____

2. Psalm 16:9–11

_____

_____

_____

_____

_____

_____

_____

_____

_____

_____

If you have a study Bible, it may have references in a margin, a middle column, or footnotes that point to other biblical texts. You may find it helpful in understanding how the whole story of God ties together to look up some of those other scriptures from time to time.

3. Isaiah 35

4. Isaiah 52:13–53:12

5. Ezekiel 37:1–14

6. John 20:19–23

7. Romans 6:5–10

_____

_____

_____

_____

_____

_____

8. 1 Corinthians 15

_____

_____

_____

_____

_____

_____

9. Philippians 3:7–11

_____

_____

_____

_____

_____

_____

10. Colossians 1:15–23

_____

_____

_____

_____

_____

_____

WEEK 7, DAY 5

Luke and Our World Today

When we enter into this fascinating narrative of Jesus's resurrection, this story—perhaps more than any other—becomes the lens through which we see ourselves, our world, and God's action in our world today.

1. What does the resurrection story say to us about ourselves, our world, and God's action in our world today?

It's tempting to see the resurrection, and the other stories we've been reading about in Luke,

as ancient history. But we should work to keep this story, more than any other story in the

Bible, current, fresh, and at the forefront of our minds. After all, the resurrection of Jesus

should impact how we live today. If resurrection is true, the world has been turned upside

down. The newsboy Luke has just handed us an epic flyer with the most amazing good news.

Where do we go from here?

Following the above example, answer these questions about how we can understand ourselves, our world, and God's action in our world today.

2. How is sight connected to faith over and over in the resurrection story? Why do you think this metaphor is used so often in this way?

3. In what way do you encounter the risen Jesus in the Communion meal?

_____

_____

_____

_____

_____

_____

_____

4. The resurrection is the source of the energy that drives Christian witness. How would you gauge your enthusiasm to share the good news of Luke 24?

_____

_____

_____

_____

_____

_____

_____

Invitation and Response

God's Word always invites a response. Think about the way the theme of resurrection speaks to us today. How does the story invite us to respond?

_____

_____

_____

_____

_____

Women were the
first preachers of the
gospel of Christ.